A 30 MINUTE SUMMARY OF THE KEY
CONCEPTS IN

DIRTY GENES by Dr. Ben Lynch

By High Speed Reads

D1736914

Table of Contents

Introduction: Your Genes Are Not Your Destiny

Summary

There are a great many people in the world suffering from brain and mood issues, cardiovascular issues, cancers, fertility and pregnancy issues, metabolism issues, organ issues and also female hormone issues. What the average person doesn't know is that we can support and reinforce our genes to ensure peak health. Take SNP's, single-nucleotide polymorphism, for example. The great majority of them don't alter how our bodies operate but there are some that have an immense effect on us. If SNP's are found in the MTHFR gene it can cause birth defects, cancer and irritability along with many other health problems.

Issues such as those mentioned above and many others that at one point seemed overwhelming and hopeless slowly began to make sense thanks to the research into SNP's and the breakthroughs that resulted. All of a sudden many of those issues became manageable through changes in lifestyle and diet which in turn had the effect of reshaping the gene's very behavior.

So, are we held hostage by our genes, destined to suffer from depression if our father was depressed or destined for diabetes if it runs on our mother's side of the family? No, the good news is that we get to change and edit our genes sort of like a word document, if you noticed a word that's spelled wrong you don't just leave it there you fix it and we can help fix our document by using chemical free products, eating properly, finding occasion to laugh and getting plenty of rest. While at the same time when you choose to only get 5 or less hours of sleep per night, use products loaded with chemicals and allow stress to control your life your adding more and more errors to your document which when combined can lead to health problems.

A few common symptoms of dirty genes are brain fog, anxiety, cold feet and hands, depression, nosebleeds, itchy skin, fatigue, irritability, attention problems, rosacea, difficult periods/pms, aching muscles/joints, acid reflux, indigestion, fibromyalgia, cravings for sugar and carbs, allergic reactions and gallstones.

With that being said get ready to begin the journey of cleaning your dirty genes, within these pages you will find out how you can make the most of the genes you were born with, how to clean them and how to keep them clean. In no time you should notice a better feeling, healthier and happier you.

Recap of Introduction:

1. Most SNP's don't alter how our bodies operate but there are some that have an immense effect on us.
2. Thanks to research into SNP's many health issues that were once seen as overwhelming have become manageable with lifestyle and diet changes.
3. We are not held hostage by our genes, we can edit them in such a way that we can reach a healthier and happier version of ourselves.
4. Common symptoms of dirty genes include brain fog, anxiety, cold feet and hands, depression, irritability, aching joints and gallstones among others.

Chapter 1: Cleaning Up Your Dirty Genes

Summary

It should come as no surprise that the way to reach peak health is by supporting your genes. To begin with let's talk about the 2 types of dirty genes, those born dirty and those simply acting dirty. Genetic polymorphism is the scientific term for a born dirty gene, their also called SNP's. Born dirty genes help decide if you will be optimistic or depressed, slim or heavy, energized or sluggish, calm or anxious. Within this book were going to focus on the 7 genes most likely to impact your health and the SNP's that effect them.

On the other hand some genes simply act dirty. There are many reasons for a gene to act dirty, perhaps you're under too much stress or using too many chemicals, perhaps you're not getting enough sleep or your genes could be getting too few nutrients. How your genes react to your environment, mindset, lifestyle and diet is called genetic expression. If your genes act dirty enough, even without SNP's present, you can face such serious conditions as heart disease, cancer, diabetes or autoimmune disorders. Conversely if your genes have the lifestyle and diet they need to thrive you'll be able to enhance your life, your mental outlook and most importantly your health.

Now let me introduce you to the seven genes we'll be focusing on. If these happen to be dirty, acting or born, then you can be sure the rest of your genes are in rough shape too.

- **MTHFR**- This gene influences your stress response, energy production, inflammation, brain chemistry, detoxification, immune response, genetic expression, cell repair and antioxidant production.
- **COMT**- This gene along with its SNP's hold a strong influence on your mood, on your ability to focus, on

how your body handles estrogen and it's even a key factor in the menstrual cycle.

- **DAO**- When this gene is dirty it can make you extra sensitive to certain chemicals and foods.
- **MAOA**- This gene helps manage the key brain chemicals that influence your self confidence, sleep, mood, vulnerability to addictions and alertness.
- **GST/GPX**- A dirty GST or GPX influences your body's ability to remove harmful chemicals.
- **NOS3**- This gene influences your body's production of nitric oxide, which is a big part of heart health.
- **PEMT**- This gene supports your liver, bile flow, muscle health, brain development and your cell membranes.

It might come as a shock but having dirty genes actually can have some benefits. Our goal here is to use lifestyle change, diet and limited chemical exposure to minimize the problems and maximize the benefits. Let me tell you a few more things that can dirty up your genes: deficient protein, deficient healthy fats, excessive sugar, excessive carbs, excessive protein, too few nutrients for your genes to function properly, lazy lifestyle, dehydration, overtraining, not getting enough sleep, chemicals in food/water/air and excessive physical or mental stress. From day 1 babies are born with over 200 chemicals in their bodies. This is why it's important to filter your water, clean up the air in your home, limit stress, sleep well, eat organic and avoid using chemical infused products in your hair and on your skin.

The Four Week Clean Genes Protocol is your first line of defense when it comes to supporting your genes. I'll teach you how to scrub those that are acting dirty as well as those that were born dirty until their all clean. Give it four weeks and see the difference.

Step 1: Soak and Scrub for Two Weeks (This is where we'll clean all of your genes) to begin you'll need to complete laundry list 1 in chapter 4. You'll simply be required to check which personality traits and symptoms you've noticed in yourself so we can better identify which genes aren't functioning properly. Next you'll be required to follow the 2 week program of reduced toxic exposure, stress relief, sufficient sleep and eating healthy foods. This part of the program is excellent at clearing out any toxins in your system. The soak and scrub is vital as it washes away much of the dirt from your genes so we can better see where we need to spot clean.

Step 2: Spot Clean for Two Weeks (This is where we focus on cleaning any genes that were born dirty) To begin you'll need to complete laundry list 2 in chapter 14. Here we'll be identifying which of your genes are still dirty so we can do a bit of spot cleaning. The clean genes protocol uses lifestyle and diet changes to help you reach these goals.

Step 3: Keep Clean for Life (This step requires you to continue to monitor your genes to ensure they stay healthy) You'll want to revisit that second laundry list every 3-6 months so you can identify any genes that are still causing you trouble. It's imperative that you stick to the program and follow the healthy lifestyle and diet recommendations that you're going to learn in your four week program while including the spot cleaning methods as needed.

Without further ado it's time to introduce you to your clean genes protocol. Below is an overview of the protocol and each component will be addressed in greater detail in future chapters.

Diet- Avoid late night meals and snacks. Eat healthy fats and proper amounts of protein. Avoid eating leftovers, fermented foods or foods with excess bacteria. Avoid foods with excess preservatives, pesticides, herbicides or artificial ingredients.

Remove excess carbs, white sugar, gluten and cow's milk from your diet. Stop eating when your 80% full. Be certain you get all of the nutrients your genes need to function at their best, zinc, copper, vitamin c and vitamin b. Avoid eating anything high in histamines, certain types of cheese, wine, preserved or smoked meat or fish.

Sleep- Remove or block out artificial light. Try to be consistent with your sleep schedule, asleep by 10:30pm every night and awake 8 hours later. Turn off or remove any electric screens an hour before you to go sleep. Your priority should be getting restful, deep sleep.

Exercise- Don't overdo it; exercise the right amount for your body. Make sure you're well rested before you begin any work out and be sure not to exhaust yourself. Never let exercise interrupt your sleep, if you find it does try starting an early morning routine.

Stress- Try to resolve any psychological stress you may have: Troubles at home, work or with your family or loved ones. Try to reduce any symptoms of physical stress: chronic infections, illnesses, lack of sleep or allergies.

Environmental Toxins- Filter your bathing, cooking and drinking water. Eat organic as often as possible. Try to keep your indoor air as clean as possible. Stop using garden and household chemicals. Don't use plastic containers to store your food or water. Only store and cook your food in stainless steel or glass.

This protocol has worked for my clients, my family and me. I've also taught other health care providers how to implement it with their patients. The next step is for you to learn some important facts about genetic science. These details will aid you on your journey.

6

1. There are 2 types of dirty genes, those born dirty and those simply acting dirty.
2. Born dirty genes help decide if you will be optimistic or depressed, slim or heavy, energized or sluggish, calm or anxious.
3. There are many reasons for a gene to act dirty, perhaps your under too much stress or using too many chemicals, perhaps you're not getting enough sleep or your genes could be getting too few nutrients.
4. How your genes react to your environment, mindset, lifestyle and diet is called genetic expression
5. It's important to filter your water, clean up the air in your home, limit stress, sleep well, eat organic and avoid using chemical infused products in your hair and on your skin.
6. From day 1 babies are born with over 200 chemicals in their bodies

Chapter 2: Gene Secrets: What they didn't teach you in science class

Summary

Supporting Methylation is one of the primary goals of the clean genes protocol. Methlyation's purpose is to determine if a gene should be turned off or turned on, in other words it has control over your genetic expression. If you're dealing with pms, acne, headaches, diabetes, heart disease or obesity your body is most likely not methylating properly. It's important that you support your liver as nearly 85% of Methlyation occurs there. A few tips would be to avoid heavy metals in your food, air and water. Also avoid recreational drug use and drink alcohol sparingly. When Methylation is working properly you reduce the odds of getting anxiety, depression, dementia, obesity, heart disease, cancer and autoimmune conditions. Methylation has the power to change the information your genes send out.

Let's take a look at some of the other ways Methylation helps us. It produces phosphatidylcholine which is an important element of your cell walls. If your cell walls aren't working properly it won't matter what supplements or vitamins you take they will never make it to your cells. Methylation makes muscle and brain food in the form of creatine. Methylation helps to remove excess hormones and dangerous chemicals from your body. It also helps your immune system find a harmonious balance, not too active and not too passive. When new cells are born Methylation helps avert DNA errors and it's crucial for DNA repair.

Now that we know how important Methylation is, what causes it to go wrong? A few examples are a poor diet, getting too much folic acid in your diet, over exercising, poor sleep habits, too much stress, being exposed to harmful chemicals, alcohol, heavy metals, inflammation, infections and antacids. The clean genes protocol is designed to support the Methylation process by ensuring you get a deep sleep, the right amount of exercise, a reduction of stress, a diet filled with methyl donors and nutrients and also that you avoid heavy metals and chemicals.

Recap of Chapter 2:

1. Methlyation's purpose is to determine if a gene should be turned off or turned on, in other words it has control over your genetic expression
2. 85% of Methylation occurs in your liver.
3. Methylation helps to remove excess hormones and dangerous chemicals from your body.
4. When new cells are born Methylation helps avert DNA errors
5. The clean genes protocol is designed to support the Methylation process by ensuring you get a deep sleep, the right amount of exercise, a reduction of stress and a diet filled with methyl donors.

Summary

It's been mentioned that when you support your genes with proper exercise, the right diet, stress relief and reduced chemical exposure your born dirty genes become significantly more manageable. Unfortunately stress has the opposite effect and since we all deal with stress at one point or another it's important to keep our stress levels in check. The clean genes protocol is so effective because it cleans ALL of your genes and then gives you the tools to spot clean those that need extra work. Keeping your genes operating at their optimal levels is possible with a little work and a lifestyle and diet change.

Let's take another look at the 7 genes we'll be focused on.

- **MTHFR**: Aids the methylation process
- **COMT**: Influences the metabolism of norepinephrine, dopamine and epinephrine, affecting your energy level, mood, sleep quality and focus.
- **DAO**: Influences your body's reaction to histamine from bacteria and food which affects your susceptibility to food intolerance and allergy symptoms.
- **MAOA**: Influences your connection to serotonin, dopamine and norepinephrine which manages your carb cravings, sleep quality, mood and energy level.
- **GST/GPX**: Initiates detoxification.
- **NOS3**: Helps with circulation which is needed for heart health.
- **PEMT**: Influences your brain, liver and cell walls. Determines if you will have gallstones, pregnancy problems, SIBO, attention problems or fatty liver.

So what should your takeaway be from this information? Keep your genes clean at all times, make it a daily goal. Determine which genes need more support and help them as best as you can. If you're interested in learning your genetic profile you can get tested by 23andMe or Genos Research. With the information they provide you will know where any SNP's are hiding. Another option would be to simply take 4 weeks and complete the Clean Genes Protocol. The choice is yours. The bottom line is that to keep your genes in optimal condition you must continue with the Clean Genes Protocol, dedicate yourself to a lifelong, lifestyle change. The end results will be a happier healthier life.

Recap of Chapter 3:

1. when you support your genes with proper exercise, the right diet, stress relief and reduced chemical exposure your born dirty genes become significantly more manageable
2. Keep your genes clean at all times, make it a daily goal. Determine which genes need more support and help them as best as you can
3. If you're interested in learning your genetic profile you can get tested by 23andMe or Genos Research.

Chapter 4: Laundry List 1: Which of Your Genes Need Cleaning?

Summary

Now it's time to get excited, Your about to complete the first laundry list which encompasses a range of symptoms. The purpose of completing this list is to identify which genes are dirty so you can begin making changes for the better. Take your time and be honest with yourself as the results will show us if your diet, nutrition, lifestyle, mindset or environment are negatively influencing your genes. All you have to do is check the box if the condition has occurred frequently within the last 2 months:

DAO:

- o I suffer from leaky gut syndrome and my system is sensitive to many types of food.
- o I often feel better several hours after a meal as opposed to 15-20 minutes after a meal.
- o My system is sensitive to Alcohol or red wine.
- o When I eat fish, citrus or leftovers I suffer from nosebleeds, runny nose, headache, sweatiness and/or irritability.
- o During pregnancy I felt great and could eat diverse types of foods with no problems.

COMT(Slow):

- o My body is very sensitive to pain.
- o I get headaches easily.
- o Falling asleep is difficult for me.
- o I get PMS.
- o I'm often irritable or anxious.

COMT(Fast):

- I often feel depressed.
- I'm not very motivated.
- I don't do well with focus or attention
- I have an addictive personality: smoking, alcohol, shopping, gaming, social media.
- I feel great after eating starchy foods or carbs but the feeling of depression returns fast.

MTHFR:

- I often have cold feet and hands.
- I often feel depressed
- When I exercise I sweat profusely.
- I get headaches easily.
- I eat food high in folic acid or I take folic acid supplements.

MAOA(Slow):

- I don't fall asleep fast but once I'm asleep I tend to sleep well.
- I get headaches or migraines easily.
- After getting irritated or stressed I find it difficult to calm down.
- After eating chocolate, cheese and/or wine I tend to feel irritable.
- It's typical for me to be anxious, stressed or panicked.

MAOA(Fast):

- Eating chocolate tends to boost my mood.
- I suffer from a lack of desire and I often feel depressed.
- I get to sleep fast but tend to wake up too early.
- I drink alcohol or smoke to excess. To the point of addiction.
- After eating carbohydrates I tend to be in a good mood but I lack attention or focus.

GST/GPX:

o   I noticed gray hairs early.
o   I suffer from diabetes, eczema, psoriasis, asthma, inflammatory bowel disease, autoimmune disease or another chronic condition.
o   My body doesn't tolerate chemicals well.
o   I suffer from seizures, problems with gait, tremors, tics or other neurological disorders.

NOS3:

o   I suffer from type 2 diabetes.
o   I often have cold feet and hands.
o   My blood pressure is often high. (above 120/80)
o   I am postmenopausal.
o   After surgery or an injury my body tends to heal slowly.

PEMT:

o   My gallbladder was removed/ I suffer from gallstones.
o   I suffer from SIBO, small intestine bacterial overgrowth.
o   I often have pain in my muscles.
o   I suffer from fatty liver.
o   I'm vegan or vegetarian / I don't eat caviar, eggs, organ meat or beef very often.

Great job, now let's get you scored. Each gene should have its own score; you will be allocating 1 point per question you checked.

0 points: Awesome, this gene is most likely clean and doing great.

1 point: Pretty good but this gene most likely needs some attention.

2 points: This gene is somewhat dirty; following the clean genes protocol should get rid of the gunk.

3-5 points: This gene is very dirty; following the clean genes protocol for 2 weeks is a great start but you should complete laundry list 2 to determine if it needs further attention.

Your Score:

DAO ___

COMT(Slow)___

COMT(Fast)___

MTHFR___

MAOA(Slow)___

MAOA(Fast)___

GST/GPX___

NOS3___

PEMT___

The next 7 chapters will go into great detail about each of the 7 key genes we've been covering. Regardless of your score for a particular gene it's important that you read every chapter in this book. The instructions your genes give every second of every day mold your personality, your body and your health. Your genes are the building blocks of your life. With that said let's keep moving.

Recap of Chapter 4:

1. The purpose of completing this list is to identify which genes are dirty so you can start making changes for the better.

2. Take your time and be honest with yourself as the results will show us if your diet, nutrition, lifestyle, mindset or environment are negatively influencing your genes.

3. Don't feel bad if you have lots of dirty genes, that just means you have lots of potential to improve your health.

Chapter 5: MTHFR: Methylation Master

Summary

If you completed the laundry list in the previous chapter you should know if your MTHFR gene is dirty or not. MTHFR is important to the Methylation cycle and if it's dirty it can cause your mental outlook to deteriorate, your energy to drop, your hormones can go crazy, heart troubles and even your metabolism can be negatively affected. So how do you fix this? One way is to eat lots of leafy greens (lightly cooked greens and salads) since their full of methylfolate. Methylfolate is the biochemical that's used to jump start the Methylation cycle. You can also take a Methylfolate supplement to give your recovery a head start.

A few health conditions caused by or related to a dirty MTHRF include migraines, male infertility, leukemia, high blood pressure, gastric cancer, epilepsy, blood clots, fibromyalgia, heart murmurs, autism, asthma, stroke, multiple sclerosis, thyroid cancer, vascular dementia and Parkinson's disease. A dirty MTHRF can also cause birth defects such as spina bifida, cleft palate, anencephaly and birth related complications such as preeclampsia, placental abruption, miscarriage and postpartum depression.

Next let's take a look at one of the most crucial nutrient's to the MTHFR gene, **Riboflavin**. Without Riboflavin the MTHFR gene can't operate properly and if the gene is dirty it will require even more Riboflavin. So how can you help? Be certain your getting enough Riboflavin in your daily diet through foods like almonds, spinach, wild salmon, eggs, lamb, mushroom and liver. Without Riboflavin your MTHFR gene won't be able to start the Methylation cycle and this will have negative consequences to your body. Other key nutrients of the Methylation cycle and the MTHFR gene include **Magnesium** (whole grains, fish, beans, avocados, nuts and leafy greens), **Folate/B9** (squash, peas, lentils, green vegetables), **Protein** (seeds, broccoli, nuts, peas, lentils, fish, lamb, beef, poultry, eggs and dairy), **Cobalamin/B12** (Crab, eggs, salmon, clams, red meat – vegans and vegetarians must supplement)

Recap of Chapter 5:

1. MTHFR is important to the Methylation cycle and if its dirty it can cause your mental outlook to deteriorate, your energy to drop, your hormones can go crazy, heart troubles and even your metabolism can be negatively affected.
2. Methylfolate is the biochemical that's used to jump start the Methylation cycle
3. Without Riboflavin the MTHFR gene can't operate properly and if the gene is dirty it will require even more Riboflavin.
4. 5 key nutrients to the Methylation cycle and your MTHFR gene include Riboflavin, Magnesium, Folate/B9, Protein and Cobalamin/B12.

Summary

Your COMT gene controls your body's ability to process several major neurotransmitters (norepinephrine, epinephrine and dopamine) and also estrogen and catechols. Catechols are found in coffee, black tea, chocolate and green spices like thyne, parsley and peppermint. Neurotransmitters allow us to process emotions and thoughts. Let's take a look at the 3 mentioned above. Norepinephrine and Epinephrine are both stress neurotransmitters. They help when you need extra emotional or physical effort to get past an obstacle. The Dopamine neurotransmitter focuses on thrills, uncertainty and excitement. A dopamine rush can make you feel terrific, think of riding a rollercoaster, gambling or any sort of uncertain high stakes activity.

A few health conditions caused by or related to a dirty COMT include (slow comt) breast cancer, anxiety, fibroids, ADD, acute coronary syndrome, PMS, uterine cancer, schizophrenia, fibromyalgia, parkinsons disease, preeclampsia and panic disorder. (fast comt) Learning disability, ADHD, depression, addictive disorders.

One of the COMT gene's main purposes is to methylate dopamine, changing it into norepinephrine. If your COMT is acting dirty or born dirty you could be left with a type of dopamine that's harmful to your brain called dopamine quinone. Too much dopamine can cause you to be irritable or agitated. The perfect amount will give you a boost that will help you to perform your best. We all have to find the balance that works best for us.

Next let's take a look at some of the most important nutrients for your COMT gene. Since the COMT gene depends on the methylation process that means it also depends on Riboflavin,

Magnesium, Folate, Protein and Cobalamin as mentioned in the last chapter. Magnesium is specifically important as without enough your COMT will get dirty fast. About half of all U.S. residents don't have enough magnesium in their diet so it's important to eat plenty of beans, avocados, whole grains, fish, nuts, seeds and dark leafy greens. Other than diet there are 2 other causes for a lack of magnesium: long term use of proton pump inhibitors and caffeine. Later on ill offer a few alternatives to antacids and caffeine.

Recap of Chapter 6:

1. Your COMT gene controls your body's ability to process some major neurotransmitters (norepinephrine, epinephrine and dopamine) and also estrogen and catechols.

2. Catechols are found in coffee, black tea, chocolate and green spices like thyne, parsley and peppermint.

3. Neurotransmitters allow us to process emotions and thoughts.

4. One of the COMT gene's main purposes is to methylate dopamine, changing it into norepinephrine.

5. About half of all U.S. residents don't have enough magnesium in their diet so it's important to eat plenty of beans, avocados, whole grains, fish, nuts, seeds and dark leafy greens.

Chapter 7: DAO: Oversensitivity to Foods

Summary

The main purpose of the DAO gene is to produce the DAO enzyme, which happens to be most abundant in the small intestine, kidney, colon, placenta (when one is there) and prostate. Histamine, a key biochemical, is partially processed by DAO enzymes. You can find Histamine in 2 places, outside your cells and inside your cells. The purpose of the DAO enzyme is to expel any histamine that resides outside of your cells. Too much histamine can cause your immune system to get overexcited and react badly to your own tissue and even certain foods. The right amount is a great benefit to your health.

It should come as no surprise that when you add histamine from certain foods to the histamine that's already in your guy it can cause big problems especially if your DAO is dirty. A few foods high in histamine include spinach, vinegars, bone brother, alcohol, aged cheeses, dried fruits, raw tomatoes, soured foods, smoked/canned fish, fruit juices, dried fruits, fermented foods, cured meats (corned beef, pastrami and salami) and even too much chocolate.

A few health conditions caused by or related to a dirty DAO include joint pain, vertigo, nausea, psoriasis, Parkinson's disease, anaphylaxis, irritability, arrhythmia, insomnia, eczema, heartburn, asthma, duodenal ulcer, conjunctivitis and colon adenomas. A dirty DAO can also cause itchy eyes, ringing in your ears at times, trouble falling asleep, blood pressure lower than 100/60, carsickness, migraines, skin issues such as eczema or urticaria and even sweaty feet.

Now let's take a look at some of the most important nutrients for your DAO gene. There are 2, copper and calcium. **Copper** as found in turnip greens, blackstrap molasses, asparagus, beef liver, sunflower seeds, lentils and almonds and **Calcium** as found in almonds, okra, bok choy, kale, broccoli, watercress and sheep or goat cheese. Other key food items that help are Arugula, Artichokes, Almond milk, Asparagus, sea vegetables, peas, onions, mustard greens, leeks, green beans, ginger, garlic, flax, coconut, celery, carrots, Brussels sprouts and cabbage. These foods help to balance acid generating foods.

Recap of Chapter 7:

1. The main purpose of the DAO gene is to produce the DAO enzyme.
2. The purpose of the DAO enzyme is to expel any histamine that resides outside of your cells.
3. When you add histamine from certain foods to the histamine that's already in your guy it can cause big problems especially if your DAO is dirty.
4. Copper and Calcium are 2 nutrients important to your DAO gene.

Chapter 8: MAOA: Mood Swings and Carb Cravings

Summary

The main purpose of the MAOA gene is to produce the MAOA enzyme. This enzyme helps your body process norepinephrine and dopamine. These 2 neurotransmitters help your body respond to stress. The MAOA gene can have a fast or slow profile, just like the COMT gene. A fast MAOA removes serotonin, dopamine and norepinephrine too fast which can cause a shortage in those vital neurotransmitters. A slow MAOA removes serotonin, dopamine and norepinephrine slower than normal which can leave you with an overabundance of those vital neurotransmitters.

A few health conditions caused by or related to a dirty MAOA (fast or slow) include depression, ADHD, autism, fibromyalgia, anxiety, bipolar disorder, antisocial personality disorder, Alzheimer's disease, seasonal affective disorder, migraine, irritable bowel syndrome, panic disorder, schizophrenia, Parkinson's disease and obsessive compulsive disorder.

Now let's take a look at some of the most important nutrients for your MAOA gene. There are 2, tryptophan and riboflavin. **Tryptophan** can be found in seaweed, spinach, pumpkin seeds, mushrooms, red lettuce, asparagus and turnip greens. **Riboflavin** can be found in wild salmon, eggs, liver, almonds, mushrooms, lamb and spinach. Your body prefers fresh foods over supplements so I recommend working these foods into your diet if your MAOA is dirty.

Recap of Chapter 8:

1. The main purpose of the MAOA gene is to produce the MAOA enzyme.

2. The MAOA enzyme helps your body process norepinephrine and dopamine which help your body respond to stress.
3. A fast MAOA removes serotonin, dopamine and norepinephrine too fast which can cause a shortage in those vital neurotransmitters
4. A slow MAOA removes serotonin, dopamine and norepinephrine slower than normal which can leave you with an overabundance of those vital neurotransmitters.
5. Tryptophan and Riboflavin are 2 nutrients important to your MAOA gene

Chapter 9: GST/GPX: Detox Dilemmas

Summary

The main purpose of the GST gene is to produce the GST enzyme. This enzyme helps your body transfer its primary detox agent, glutathione, to xenobiotics (such as heavy metals, herbicides, pesticides) so they can leave the body through your urine. You might have a dirty GST if you have high blood pressure, increased inflammation, if you're overweight or if you have sensitivity to chemicals. The main purpose of the GPX gene is to create the GPX enzyme. This enzyme helps your body convert hydrogen peroxide (produced when were under stress) to water so it can exit the body in your urine. You might have a dirty GPX if you notice irritability, aggression, memory problems, erratic moods, chronic fatigue or white/gray hairs.

Health conditions caused by or related to a dirty GST/GPX include vision loss, Parkinson's disease, ulcerative colitis, stroke, psoriasis, seizure, Alzheimer's disease, autism, obesity, migraine, keshan disease, infertility, cancer, chemical sensitivity, homocysteine surplus, hearing loss, heart disease, hypertension, hepatitis, depression, crohn's disease, eczema, fatigue, fibromyalgia and diabetes types 1 and 2.

Next let's take a look at some of the most important nutrients for your GST/GPX genes. There are 3, Cysteine, Riboflavin and Selenium. **Cysteine** can be found in onions, asparagus, artichoke, cabbage, cauliflower, broccoli, chicken, turkey, eggs, sunflower seeds and red meat. **Riboflavin** can be found in eggs, almonds, wild salmon, mushrooms, spinach, lamb and liver. **Selenium** can be found in brown rice, eggs, beef, liver, chicken, sardines, halibut, tuna and Brazil nuts.

25

Recap of Chapter 9:

1. The main purpose of the GST gene is to produce the GST enzyme.
2. The GST enzyme helps your body transfer its primary detox agent, glutathione, to xenobiotics (such as heavy metals, herbicides, pesticides) so they can leave the body through your urine.
3. The main purpose of the GPX gene is to create the GPX enzyme.
4. The GPX enzyme helps your body convert hydrogen peroxide (produced when were under stress) to water so it can exit the body in your urine.
5. Cysteine, Riboflavin and Selenium are 3 nutrients important to your GST/GPX genes.

Summary

The main purpose of the NOS3 gene is to influence the creation of nitric oxide. Nitric oxide is extremely important to heart health because it affects blood vessel formation and blood flow. Signs that your NOS3 gene might be dirty include cold hands and feet, anxiety, angina, heart attack, depression, high blood pressure, erectile dysfunction, sinus congestion, migraines and slow healing wounds. The main way your NOS3 gets dirty is chemical exposure. It's possible to see NOS3 interacting with your brain chemistry, If your exposed to any sort of chemicals see if your mood is affected at all. We can't see the affects to our circulatory system but we can view the changes in our mood.

A few health conditions caused by or related to a dirty NOS3 include stroke, pulmonary hypertension, snoring, sleep apnea, schizophrenia, asthma, atherosclerosis, bipolar disorder, prostate cancer, preeclampsia, obesity, myocardial infarction, neurological disorders such as ALS, chronic kidney failure, recurring miscarriage, inflammation, hypertension, diabetic retinopathy, type 1 and 2 diabetes, coronary artery disease, chronic sinus congestion, carotid artery disease, breast cancer and brain ischemia.

So what can we do to help keep our NOS3 gene clean? For starters we can make sure our other genes are clean as NOS3 is particularly sensitive to other dirty genes. Second we can provide a steady supply of clean **BH4**, creating BH4 requires zinc, magnesium and folate and it's impossible to get BH4 from food so we need to maintain our MTHFR gene which helps produce BH4. Third your body needs adequate **arginine** which can be found in lentils, chickpeas, pumpkin seeds, spirulina, turkey breast, pork loin and chicken. Fourth your body needs **calcium** as found in dark leafy greens, green beans, almonds, okra, broccoli, bok choy and goat/sheep milk products. Fifth your body needs **Iron** as found in dark leafy greens, chicken liver, oysters, mussels, cashews, pine nuts, hazelnuts and beef/lamb. Sixth your body needs **Riboflavin** as found in eggs, wild salmon, spinach, almonds, mushrooms, liver and lamb. Lastly your NOS3 requires **oxygen** which you get by simply breathing.

Recap of Chapter 10:

1. The main purpose of the NOS3 gene is to influence the creation of nitric oxide.
2. Nitric oxide is extremely important to heart health because it affects blood vessel formation and blood flow.
3. The main way your NOS3 gets dirty is chemical exposure.
4. To stay clean your NOS3 gene requires BH4, Arginine, Calcium, Iron, Riboflavin, oxygen and it helps a lot for your other genes to be clean as well.

Chapter 11: PEMT: Cell Membrane and Liver Problems

Summary

The main job of the PEMT gene is the production of phosphatidylcholine, the job of which is to keep your cell membranes healthy and fluid which lets them operate at their peak level. Without phosphatidylcholine your cell membranes could become unhealthy, stiff or nonfunctional. If that happens they won't be able to transfer nutrients into your cells or move dangerous compounds out of your cells. Without its membrane your cell dies, if you remove the nucleus from a cell it will live a while longer but if the membrane is removed it dies fast. Your PEMT gene might be dirty if you have a born dirty PEMT SNP that's not responding to estrogen, insufficient estrogen, dirty MTHFR, a non functioning methylation cycle or a lack of choline or methylfolate in your diet.

A few health conditions caused by or related to a dirty PEMT gene include SIBO, muscle damage, nutrient deficiency inside your cells, birth defects, depression, breast cancer, fatigue, gallstones, liver damage and fatty liver. When your PEMT gene is dirty your body can't produce enough phosphatidylcholine and all of the many processes within your body that depend on phosphatidylcholine can't operate properly. As you can see your PEMT gene is very important to your overall health and well being.

Now let's take a look at the most important nutrient for your PEMT gene. It's called dietary **choline** which is found in red meat, chicken, fish, eggs and liver. Obviously it will be difficult for vegans and vegetarians to get dietary choline so they are at a much higher risk of being choline deficient. If you're a vegetarian or vegan you can try other sources of choline like spinach, quinoa, shitake mushrooms, pinto beans, asparagus, broccoli, beets, cauliflower, flaxseed, lentils, green peas and mung beans. One final note, research has proven that mothers who consumed greater levels of choline while pregnant had babies with improved learning abilities and improved memories while mothers who lacked choline while pregnant tended to have babies with decreased learning abilities and decreased memory.

Recap of Chapter 11:

1. The main job of the PEMT gene is the production of phosphatidylcholine.
2. Phosphatidylcholine's job is to keep your cell membranes healthy and fluid which lets them operate at their peak level.
3. Without its membrane your cell dies, if you remove the nucleus from a cell it will live a while longer but if the membrane is removed it dies fast.
4. Vegans and vegetarians are at a much higher risk of being choline deficient.
5. Research has proven that mothers who consumed greater levels of choline while pregnant had babies with improved learning abilities and improved memories while mothers who lacked choline while pregnant tended to have babies with decreased learning abilities and decreased memory

Chapter 12: Soak and Scrub: Your First Two Weeks

Summary

As humans we tend to correct what we can see and disregard everything else. The problem with this approach is that your weight gain, insomnia, rashes and headaches are caused by dirty genes and simply taking pills doesn't fix the problem, it just puts a band-aid on it. Those issues will continue to pop up as long as you ignore the root cause. In this section were going to focus on what your genes need to operate at their peak performance and for the next 2 weeks you're going to focus on giving it to them. Let's begin with week 1 of the soak and scrub. We'll cover food, supplements, detoxification, sleep and stress relief.

Soak and Scrub Week 1

Food: When discussing food the first thing I want you to know is the difference between hunger and cravings. Hunger is when your stomach growl's and feels empty and you know you need to eat. Cravings are a feeling that you want to eat a specific item. It can be difficult to know the difference when you're actively craving something but it's important to make the distinction. It's also important that you don't feel regretful or guilty if you should give in to those cravings, simply regroup and go back to the good habits you've been working on.

One step in the right direction is to plan out your meals. Food should be nurturing and restorative but that's not how most of us see it. Most of us just follow our cravings to whatever crunchy, chewy, fatty, sweet or salty item that happens to be on our minds. Try thinking of food as the fuel that makes your body go, not a bothersome chore that we need to check off a list. Food can be a beautiful part of our day if we choose to see it that way.

When planning out your meals you should take a few things into account such as your emotions that day, your activity level, any symptoms you might have and of course any genes that need cleaning. Being alert to what your body needs will go a long way in helping your genes and your overall health. Another good idea is to track your meals with a food journal or an app like CRON-O-Meter, this way when problems manifest you can identify what might have caused those issues.

Here are a few tips if you're eating to clean your genes:

- Eating organic can be highly beneficial to your genes but I know the cost can be prohibitive. If that's stopping you from eating organic then you can at least buy organic for the worst of the worst, any fruits and veggies that are high in toxins. You can find a list of the "clean" and "dirty" foods on the Environmental Working Group's website (www.ewg.org).
- If you're not hungry, simply don't eat.
- Only eat until your 80% full.
- Only eat 3 meals per day then stop. This means no snacks.
- Try fasting for 12-16 hours per day. You can do this easily if you stop eating at 7pm then start again in time for breakfast at 7am.
- Make sure you chew your food completely.
- Limit drinking while you're eating and avoid cold drinks while eating all together. Your body has to use energy to warm the drink up.
- If your running a fever you shouldn't be eating, just take electrolytes.
- Avoid drinking fruit juices and soda's, its pure sugar.
- Avoid food with ingredients you can't easily say and foods that are white.

- Focus on foods that don't have added ingredients, natural foods like fresh vegetables, some fresh fruits, nuts and seeds, wild rice, quinoa, fresh fish, free range meats and organic eggs.
- You should steam or cook your food fresh. Avoid eating left over's and frozen foods.
- When cooking be sure to use the fan, the less oil smoke you breathe in the better.

Supplements: Ideally we'd like to get all of our nutrients from food, unfortunately were not always able to do that. Nutrients are often lost due to temperature extremes, the cooking process and even transportation. Also on a daily basis were exposed to stress and chemicals that run through our nutrient supplies, for those reasons and more sometime we might need to use supplements.

Let's look at a few basic principles when choosing supplements:

- The easiest form of supplements for your body to absorb is liquid, the hardest is tablets.
- Start by taking a small dose of any supplement to see how it affects you.
- When taking multiple supplements start out 1 at a time to see how each affects you. Don't take the next supplement until you know whether the first provided a benefit or not.
- Always follow the pulse method, take the supplement while your body needs support then stop when you feel good. You don't want to end up with any excess that might cause your body to show new symptoms.
- If you're sick, not sleeping well or stressed a few supplements that might help are Electrolytes, Adaptogens and a Multivitamin without folic acid.

Detoxification: Next we'll go over a few important points on detoxification.

- Avoid plastics when cooking, eating from or storing food. This applies to cups as well.
- Instead use clay, glass or stainless steel for any of your cooking or eating needs.
- Don't use scented products like air fresheners, soaps, toilet paper, dryer sheets or paper towels.
- Don t use nonstick cookware or pans.
- Stay away from insecticides, herbicides and pesticides.
- Know your surroundings. Check for toxins like mold or mildew, Look for damp areas and water spots on the ceiling or floor, and be sure to clean up and remove any found.
- Sweating is a good thing, try wearing warm clothes, walking fast, exercise or taking an Epsom salt bath. A sauna or hot yoga are options if you're taking electrolytes. Make sure you wash with soap and water after. Don't stay in a sauna longer than you need to, once you've had enough, leave.

Sleep: Let's take a look at a few important sleep factors.

- Try improving the quality of your sleep by not eating 3 hours before bedtime, turning off any lights, drinking no caffeine after 2pm, stopping any electronic activity an hour before bedtime and perhaps instill a blue light filter for your phone or computer.
- The perfect bedtime is 10:30 p.m. so if you stay up much later than that you should start making some changes. Perhaps try getting to sleep a half hour earlier every other night, then every night.

Stress Relief: We all experience stress so here are a few suggestions to get those feelings under control.

- Try doing an easy stretching routine for 5-10 minutes every day.

- Get outside and enjoy the day by playing sports, meeting friends or just going for a walk.
- Try some deep breathing exercises. There are many free app's, android and apple, that will walk you through guided meditation or breathing exercises.

Soak and Scrub week 2

You will want to continue to follow the steps from week 1 but now we can add/change a few items for week 2.

Food: This week I really want you to focus on eating in peace, if you're eating alone enjoy the silence and focus on the food, if you're with family or friends enjoy good conversation. Remove any electronics from the table and focus on the moment.

Supplements: If you're already taking a multivitamin I'd like you to add in a new nutrient, liposomal glutathione. If your armpits, breathe or gas smell like sulfur you can take molybdenum. If you're experiencing bloating or belching after or during meals try taking betaine hydrochloride with pancreatic enzymes. If you have a stomach ulcer you should avoid taking any digestive enzymes until it's healed.

Detoxification: Continue to avoid household cleaners, instead use vinegar, baking soda, salt, hot water and other basics. If you don't already have one you should get a multistage water filter. Add a filter to your shower that will remove any chlorine from you water. Give it a week; you'll notice that your hair and skin feel a lot better. If you have carpet in your home you should be using a HEPA filter vacuum. Regular vacuum's spread more dust around than they pick up. Next clean your air ducts and your furnace air filters. Lastly clean the pipes that are under your sink, you'll need to take them apart and scrub the inside with hot soapy water, also clean out the sink traps.

Sleep: If you're not in bed by 10:30pm yet you should continue to inch towards that goal. Also try to rise with the sun; you can purchase a sunrise alarm clock to help create morning light.

Stress Relief: You should limit your social media intake, a few times per day is fine but not more than that. Try to limit your news intake, fasting from news and any negative conversations will do wonders. Focus on limiting the amount of negative information you feed your brain. Lastly try meditating for at least 3-5 minutes every night before you go to bed. As mentioned previously there are apps that can help with this.

Be Thorough during your 2 week soak and scrub.

Make a promise to yourself that for 2 weeks you will commit to following these guidelines. If you want to feel better and heal your body it will take action and commitment. Chapter 15 discusses spot cleaning but I don't want you to worry about that until you've taken the 2 week soak and scrub as far as you can. If you think you need more than 2 weeks feel free to stay on it for as long as you continue to see improvements. If you sincerely give the soak and scrub a chance I know after the 2 weeks are up you'll feel significantly better and so will your genes.

Recap of Chapter 12:

1. your weight gain, insomnia, rashes and headaches are caused by dirty genes and simply taking pills doesn't fix the problem, it just puts a band-aid on it
2. Hunger is when your stomach growl's and feels empty and you know you need to eat. Cravings are a feeling that you want to eat a specific item
3. Nutrients are often lost due to temperature extremes, the cooking process and even transportation.
4. The easiest form of supplements for your body to absorb is liquid, the hardest is tablets

5. Check for toxins like mold or mildew, Look for damp areas and water spots on the ceiling or floor, and be sure to clean up and remove any found
6. Try improving the quality of your sleep by not eating 3 hours before bedtime, turning off any lights, drinking no caffeine after 2pm, stopping any electronic activity an hour before bedtime and perhaps instill a blue light filter for your phone or computer.
7. Try some deep breathing exercises. There are many free app's, android and apple, that will walk you through guided meditation or breathing exercises.

Chapter 13: Your Clean Genes Recipes

Summary

If you want food to be your medicine then you must eat healthy, supportive and clean foods. I recommend you use only filtered water when cooking and buy only organic ingredients. Typical fish, meats and produce will only make your genes dirty just like unfiltered water. Also you should be using Celtic or Himalayan sea salt instead of regular table salt. These 2 alternatives are high in minerals.

Back in chapter 4 we went over the laundry list 1 and in chapter 14 you'll be introduced to laundry list 2. By completing these lists you will have a good idea of which of your genes is dirty, then you can focus on foods that help strengthen those genes. The following tips will benefit anyone regardless of what genes are dirty, we'll focus on helping specifics genes after. Let's begin.

- You should stop eating once your 80% full.
- Try to eat only 3 meals per day without snack sin between.
- Try a daily fasting routine, 12-16 hours daily of no food.
- Make sure you're calm and relaxed when you decide to eat.
- Remove any distractions while eating like your phone or laptop. Focus on the food or conversation.
- Only eat when you're truly hungry, not when you have a craving.
- Avoid eating 3 hours before you go to bed.
- Make sure your meals include a balance of fats, carbs and protein.
- If possible only consume organically grown foods.

Now let's move on to food that targets your specific dirty genes.

Dirty MTHFR: Focus on recipes and foods with beans and leafy greens. Also any recipe that helps to support your PEMT gene.

Slow COMT, Slow MAOA: Make sure your breakfast includes a balance of fat, carbs and protein. Your lunch should include a balance of fat, protein and salad. Your dinner should include a small amount of protein with more fat and salad.

Fast COMT, Fast MAOA: Make sure your breakfast includes a balance of fats, carbs and protein. Your lunch should also include a balance of fats, carbs and protein. Your dinner should include a balance of fats, carbs and protein as well.

Dirty DAO: You shouldn't be eating any leftovers, only newly prepared foods. Make sure any meat or seafood you eat is rinsed and dried before cooking and fresh. You should focus on recipes with low histamine ingredients and recipes where you can reduce the amount of histamine ingredients that are used.

Dirty GST/GPX: You should focus on any recipe with leafy greens, eggs, cruciferous vegetables or salads.

Dirty NOS3: You should focus on recipes that include seeds and nuts. Also any recipe that supports your PEMT, MTHFR, and GST genes. Any recipe that helps to balance your MAOA and COMT genes is also beneficial for a dirty NOS3.

Dirty PEMT: You should focus on recipes that include lamb, quinoa, beets and eggs. You can include any recipes that benefit your MTHFR gene.

Recap of Chapter 13:

1. If you want food to be your medicine then you must eat healthy, supportive and clean foods.
2. Use only filtered water when cooking and buy only organic ingredients for cooking.
3. Typical fish, meats and produce will only make your genes dirty just like unfiltered water.
4. You should be using Celtic or Himalayan sea salt instead of regular table salt. These 2 alternatives are high in minerals

Chapter 14: Laundry List 2: Which Genes Need More Cleaning?

Summary

If you've made it this far that means it's time to start laundry list number 2. You should only complete this laundry list after you've completed the 2 week soak and scrub. That way we can determine which of your genes will need more attention and which are doing better. Fill out the following questionnaire and be as honest as possible, remember you're only hurting yourself by being dishonest, and then score each gene independently. Those scores can then be used to see which genes need more help or spot cleaning.

Check the box if the condition has occurred regularly within the last 2 months:

MTHFR:

- o After exercising I become red in the face or have shortness of breath.
- o Sometimes exercising triggers my asthma.
- o My mood switches between depressed and irritable.
- o My body doesn't handle alcohol of any type very well.
- o My body often feels "toxic" and tired.
- o I should be eating leafy green vegetables daily but I don't.
- o If I'm not sad or upset I'm able to concentrate/focus very well.
- o Falling asleep remains difficult for me.
- o While at the dentist I've been given nitrous oxide and I felt terrible.
- o If I'm upset it takes me a while to settle back down.
- o On some days I'm a risk taker but on most I play it safe.

DAO:

- After eating I often feel itchy, hot or irritable.
- My body doesn't tolerate alcohol, citrus, fish, wine, cheese or yogurt well.
- Sometimes I get erratic joint pains that seem to move around.
- I suffer from psoriasis, eczema, urticaria or other skin issues.
- I get red streaks if I scratch my skin.
- My body can't handle probiotics.
- I suffer from SIBO.
- I suffer from many food intolerances and food allergies.
- Sometimes I get a ringing in my ears, often after eating.
- I suffer from Crohn's disease, ulcerative colitis or leaky gut syndrome.
- I often get headaches/migraines.
- I often get nose bloods or a runny nose.
- It can take me hours to get to sleep after I eat or sleep.
- I suffer from exercise triggered asthma or regular asthma.

COMT (Slow):

- After eating a high-protein diet I tend to have a short temper.
- I tend to get annoyed easily and it takes a while for me to settle back down.
- I regularly get PMS.
- I'm usually very happy but I tend to have a short fuse.
- I don't have much patience.
- I can stay focused or study for hours just fine.
- I've had trouble falling asleep since I was a kid.
- I was put on birth control to get heavy bleeding or acne under control.

- I currently or previously suffered from uterine fibroids.
- Caffeine keeps me alert but if I drink too much I get grumpy.
- I'm very prudent by nature and prefer not to take risks.

COMT (Fast):

- I often find it difficult to focus.
- On most days I feel depressed.
- I'm able to calm down pretty fast if I'm stressed.
- I'm usually calm but sometimes I wish I wasn't so calm all the time.
- I like taking risks. I enjoy how I feel after.
- I like making people smile, some might call me the class clown.
- It's hard for me to keep still, I'm usually fidgeting.
- I've been known to pinch myself, hard.
- I'm not a morning person.
- I have an addictive personality: smoking, shopping, video games, drugs etc.
- Sex doesn't really interest me.
- At night I typically fall asleep almost instantly.
- When I need to pay attention caffeine does the trick to help me focus.
- High sugar foods tend to give me a mood boost, also foods high in fat. The boost doesn't last that long though.

MAOA (Slow):

- I'm often rather hostile to other people.
- It usually takes me some time to calm down.
- I'm able to focus for long periods of time.
- I typically become an angry drunk when drinking alcohol.

- I feel less annoyed when I'm not eating carbs, I don't tend to crave them.
- When I drink wine or eat chocolate or cheese I tend to get annoyed easily.
- I don't fall asleep easily.
- When I do fall asleep I don't wake up until morning.
- I have depression and was prescribed an SSRI and it makes me extremely bad tempered.
- Melatonin doesn't make me sleepy; instead it makes me feel irritable.
- I usually feel irritable after taking caffeine.
- If I'm in a bad mood Lithium tends to help.
- When I take 5-HTP I tend to feel irritable and anxious.
- I get over stimulated when I take inositol.
- I'm usually very self confident.
- I'm male.

MAOA (Fast):

- I've had a tough time paying attention and focusing since I was young.
- I often feel good after I eat chocolate, wine or cheese. I crave them.
- Carbohydrates tend to make me feel less depressed. I crave them.
- I don't often sleep through the night but I tend to fall asleep fast. A snack helps me get back to sleep.
- I suffer from an autoimmune disease. (multiple sclerosis, active celiac or graves' disease)
- I suffer from chronic inflammation.
- My mood is often affected by prolonged darkness and winter. I've been diagnosed with seasonal affective disorder.
- Exercise is great; it gives me a mood boost.
- I'm female.
- I tend to worry a lot.

- I'm often anxious and depressed.
- I tend to obsess over things.
- I suffer from irritable bowel syndrome, constipation or fibromyalgia.
- When I need to get to sleep Melatonin helps a lot.
- When I'm in a bad mood Inositol helps a lot.
- When I'm in a bad mood 5-HTP helps a lot.
- Taking Lithium causes me to become more depressed.
- Taking an SSRI has helped me.

GST/GPX:

- My body doesn't tolerate chemicals and smells very well.
- After sweating heavily or taking a sauna I feel great.
- Even though I eat right I tend to gain weight easily.
- Many people in my family have been diagnosed with cancer.
- When I'm going through a stressful period I notice white or gray hairs coming in.
- My hair has started to gray early.
- I suffer from high blood pressure.
- My body recently fought off an infection.
- I'm usually stressed out over something.
- I suffer from an autoimmune disorder.
- I suffer from chronic inflammation.
- I sometimes have difficulty breathing or I have asthma and often feel as though I can't get enough air.
- My body often feels toxic or tired.

NOS3:

- I suffer from high blood pressure.
- I've had 1 or more heart attacks.
- I suffer from type 1 or type 2 diabetes.

- My feet and hands are typically cold.
- I suffer from asthma.
- I have sleep apnea, I often breathe through my mouth or I tend to snore.
- My memory has been getting worse lately.
- During my pregnancy I had preeclampsia.
- I suffer from atherosclerosis.
- I'm currently post menopausal.
- I tend to have wild mood swings.
- On any given day I don't move around or exercise that often.
- I suffer from an autoimmune disease.
- I suffer from chronic inflammation.

PEMT:

- I'm currently post menopausal.
- I suffer from gallstones.
- I don't eat as many leafy green vegetables as I should
- I rarely eat meat or eggs.
- I've been diagnosed with a fatty liver.
- I suffer from SIBO.
- I am currently a vegan or vegetarian.
- My gallbladder was removed.
- For years now I've had pain all over my body.
- My body doesn't handle fatty foods that great.
- Halfway through a pregnancy is when my symptoms started and they've continued to get worse.
- I have low estrogen levels.
- 1 or more of my children suffers from a congenital birth defect.
- I was worn out mentally and physically by breastfeeding.

Great, now let's figure out your score. Each gene should have its own score; you will be allocating 1 point per question you checked.

0 points: Awesome, this gene is most likely clean and doing great.

1-4 points: Pretty good but this gene most likely needs some attention.

5-7 points: This gene is somewhat dirty and definitely needs some attention.

8+ points: This gene is very dirty; try to determine what is negatively affecting it. Also other genes that scored high could be negatively influencing it as well.

You're Score:

MTHFR: ___

DAO: ___

COMT (Slow): ___

COMT (Fast): ___

MAOA (Slow): ___

MAOA (Fast): ___

GST/GPX: ___

NOS3: ___

PEMT: ___

Remember your environment and your body are constantly changing, don't just finish the questionnaire and the spot cleaning and go back to your old ways. Try to form some new habits, better habits, by revisiting this second laundry list every 6 months or so to give your genes a quick checkup. I can say with confidence that the soak and scrub, the laundry list and the spot cleaning are the best methods available to keep your genes clean for your present self and also for your future self.

Recap of Chapter 14:

1. The purpose of the second laundry list is to find out which of your genes need further attention, spot cleaning, and which are doing better.
2. You should only be completing the second laundry list if you've already done the 2 week soak and scrub.
3. Try to form some new habits, better habits, by revisiting this second laundry list every 6 months or so to give your genes a quick checkup.

Chapter 15: Spot Cleaning: Your Second Two Weeks

Summary

Before we jump into the spot cleaning did you follow the soak and scrub instructions completely? If yes, that's great you're ready to move on. If not your results from the spot clean won't be as good as they potentially could have been. In order for the spot clean to work all your genes need to be pretty clean. This is important because genes work together in clusters and groups. So again if you haven't followed the soak and scrub thoroughly you should focus on that before moving on.

Also make sure you implement the pulse method, fine tuning the perfect dosage for you, with any supplements you choose to try. As with anything new there is a bit of a learning curve but with lots of practice the pulse method will become routine in no time. With that said let's begin.

Spot cleaning your DAO: There are several supplements that can benefit your DAO such as Copper, Histamine blockers, Vitamin C, Fish oil, Cell membrane supporters and buffering agents like potassium bicarbonate. You also might want to consult a physician to see if you have any infections or leaky gut. You can also look into visceral manipulation of your diaphragm, gallbladder and liver.

Spot cleaning your PEMT: There are several supplements that can benefit your PEMT such as creatine, which helps to conserve your SAMe, and Phosphatidylcholine, which helps to reinforce your cell membranes. You can also look into visceral manipulation of your diaphragm, gallbladder and liver.

Spot cleaning your GST/GPX: There are several supplements that can benefit your GST/GPX such as Liposomal glutathione, which helps deliver glutathione right into your cells which helps them to bind to compounds. Riboflavin/VitaminB2, which can turn damaged glutathione into regenerated glutathione. Selenium, without it your body can't use glutathione to remove hydrogen peroxide. Lastly detox support powders. It's also very important that you keep your environment clean and avoid dangerous chemicals, try taking an Epsom salt bath, a sauna, hot yoga or starting an exercise routine. All of which help you expel chemicals that are harmful to your GST/GPX genes. Eating lots of fiber is great for detoxification and even getting a massage or dry brushing your skin can help.

Spot cleaning your slow COMT: There are several supplements that can benefit your slow COMT such as adaptogens, magnesium, taurine, SAMe, creatine, phosphatidyl serine, phosphatidylcholine, indole-3 and DIM. You should find a distressing method that works well for you, taking a walk or breathing exercises often work. Try focusing on any stimulating work early in the day and calming activities late in the day. It would be beneficial if you found activities or games that stimulated your brain, you're a thinker so this is important or you'll get bored. It's ok to be a workaholic but you should also take some you time in the form of a vacation or doing something you enjoy. Finding a balance is key. Try taking an Epsom salt bath, a sauna, hot yoga or starting an exercise routine. You should only be using cosmetics that are low in phthalates and buying organic produce. Eat plenty of bitter vegetables like radishes or dandelions as their good for your liver.

Spot cleaning your fast COMT: There are several supplements that you can benefit your fast COMT such as NADH, adrenal cortex, tyrosine and 5-HTP. You should consider exercising or going for a run in the morning, you should also participate in activities that stimulate your brain. Try dancing, singing, debate clubs, hiking in groups, team sports, playing an instrument or any form of social activity.

Make sure you're consuming plenty of protein on a daily basis; you need it to help stay focused.

Spot cleaning your slow MAOA: There are a few supplements that can benefit your slow MAOA such as Riboflavin and Lithium. Medications and supplements that may negatively affect your slow MAOA include SSRI's, testosterone, thyroid medication, tryptopham, 5-HTP, Melatonin, tyrosine and inositol. The slow COMT recommendations might also be of benefit to you.

Spot cleaning your fast MAOA: There are a few supplements that can benefit your fast MAOA such as NADH, 5-HTP, inositol, melatonin and liposomal curcumin. You should make note of any food intolerances and inflammatory food allergies. Having lab testing done can help. Locate any habits that might be leading to inflammation and remove them, Typical causes of inflammation are improper breathing, stress, chemical exposure, poor sleep and diet. Mold and infections are common triggers for MAOA issues so it might be good to have an environmental inspector evaluate your home or office.

Spot cleaning your MTHFR: There are a few supplements that can benefit your MTHFR such as Riboflavin/ Vitamin B2 which the MTHFR gene needs to function properly. L-5-MTHF and 6S- MTHF are both good forms of methylfolate. If you notice joint paint, runny nose, irritability, anxiety, hives or insomnia you should stop taking MTHF immediately. Taking 50 milligrams of niacin in 20 minute increments (3 times max) until the side effects subside will help. You should focus on supporting your thyroid by healing your gut, avoiding chemicals, getting plenty of sleep, filtering your water, fighting infections and reducing stress. Talk to your physician to make sure your thyroid is functioning properly.

Spot cleaning your NOS3: It's important that your other genes are clean before you focus on the NOS3 gene. If you're currently fighting a known infection you should focus on fighting said infection before supplementing your NOS3. The same goes for if you have high homocysteine or if you happen to be inflamed. When you're ready for supplements you can look into PQQ, Liposomal vitamin c, liposomal glutathione and beet root powder or citrulline. They are all beneficial to your NOS3 gene. It's important that you exercise regularly even if it's just speed walking. You might want to consider breathing exercises or tai chi to help improve your breathing. Lastly a sauna twice per week is a great way to stimulate your NOS3.

Now What?

Congratulations, you've done a great job getting this far and your well on your way to achieving your clean gene goals. If you still notice trouble spots you might want to reach out to a qualified professional such as a functional medicine professional, a licensed naturopathic physician or an environmental medicine professional. These professionals will focus on finding the cause of your troubles instead of simply suppressing them.

Recap of Chapter 15:

1. You shouldn't start the spot cleaning until after you've completed the soak and scrub.
2. In order for the spot clean to work all your genes need to be pretty clean. This is important because genes work together in clusters and groups
3. If you still notice trouble spots you might want to reach out to a qualified professional such as a functional medicine professional, a licensed naturopathic physician or an environmental medicine professional

Conclusion: The Future of Gene Health

Summary

We all have to face the fact that our genes will get dirty on a daily basis, some days they will only gather dust while others they will be covered in gunk. The good news is that you now have the tools to dust off your genes or power wash them depending on your needs. You should also know why your genes get dirty now so the next step is simple, take action. It takes action to complete the 2 week soak and scrub and it takes action to initiate and complete the spot cleaning. Once you've taken that action you'll have to decide if this will be just another book on your shelf or if it will be a roadmap to the best health you've ever experienced. You can keep up with my latest updates and inform me of your progress at www.DrBenLynch.com .

Important Facts Recap

Recap of Introduction:

1. Most SNP's don't alter how our bodies operate but there are some that have an immense effect on us.
2. Thanks to research into SNP's many health issues that were once seen as overwhelming have become manageable with lifestyle and diet changes.
3. We are not held hostage by our genes; we can edit them in such a way that we can reach a healthier and happier version of ourselves.
4. Common symptoms of dirty genes include brain fog, anxiety, cold feet and hands, depression, irritability, aching joints and gallstones among others.

Recap of Chapter 1:

1. There are 2 types of dirty genes, those born dirty and those simply acting dirty.
2. Born dirty genes help decide if you will be optimistic or depressed, slim or heavy, energized or sluggish, calm or anxious.
3. There are many reasons for a gene to act dirty, perhaps your under too much stress or using too many chemicals, perhaps you're not getting enough sleep or your genes could be getting too few nutrients.
4. How your genes react to your environment, mindset, lifestyle and diet is called genetic expression
5. It's important to filter your water, clean up the air in your home, limit stress, sleep well, eat organic and

avoid using chemical infused products in your hair and on your skin.

6. From day 1 babies are born with over 200 chemicals in their bodies

Recap of Chapter 2:

1. Methlyation's purpose is to determine if a gene should be turned off or turned on, in other words it has control over your genetic expression
2. 85% of Methylation occurs in your liver.
3. Methylation helps to remove excess hormones and dangerous chemicals from your body.
4. When new cells are born Methylation helps avert DNA errors
5. The clean genes protocol is designed to support the Methylation process by ensuring you get a deep sleep, the right amount of exercise, a reduction of stress and a diet filled with methyl donors.

Recap of Chapter 3:

1. when you support your genes with proper exercise, the right diet, stress relief and reduced chemical exposure your born dirty genes become significantly more manageable
2. Keep your genes clean at all times, make it a daily goal. Determine which genes need more support and help them as best as you can
3. If you're interested in learning your genetic profile you can get tested by 23andMe or Genos Research.

Recap of Chapter 4:

1. The purpose of completing this list is to identify which genes are dirty so you can start making changes for the better.
2. Take your time and be honest with yourself as the results will show us if your diet, nutrition, lifestyle, mindset or environment are negatively influencing your genes.
3. Don't feel bad if you have lots of dirty genes, that just means you have lots of potential to improve your health.

Recap of Chapter 5:

1. MTHFR is important to the Methylation cycle and if it's dirty it can cause your mental outlook to deteriorate, your energy to drop, your hormones can go crazy, heart troubles and even your metabolism can be negatively affected.
2. Methylfolate is the biochemical that's used to jump start the Methylation cycle
3. Without Riboflavin the MTHFR gene can't operate properly and if the gene is dirty it will require even more Riboflavin.
4. 5 key nutrients to the Methylation cycle and your MTHFR gene include Riboflavin, Magnesium, Folate/B9, Protein and Cobalamin/B12.

Recap of Chapter 6:

1. Your COMT gene controls your body's ability to process some major neurotransmitters

(norepinephrine, epinephrine and dopamine) and also estrogen and catechols.

2. Catechols are found in coffee, black tea, chocolate and green spices like thyne, parsley and peppermint.

3. Neurotransmitters allow us to process emotions and thoughts.

4. One of the COMT gene's main purposes is to methylate dopamine, changing it into norepinephrine.

5. About half of all U.S. residents don't have enough magnesium in their diet so it's important to eat plenty of beans, avocados, whole grains, fish, nuts, seeds and dark leafy greens.

Recap of Chapter 7:

1. The main purpose of the DAO gene is to produce the DAO enzyme.

2. The purpose of the DAO enzyme is to expel any histamine that resides outside of your cells.

3. When you add histamine from certain foods to the histamine that's already in your guy it can cause big problems especially if your DAO is dirty.

4. Copper and Calcium are 2 nutrients important to your DAO gene.

Recap of Chapter 8:

1. The main purpose of the MAOA gene is to produce the MAOA enzyme.

2. The MAOA enzyme helps your body process norepinephrine and dopamine which help your body respond to stress.

3. A fast MAOA removes serotonin, dopamine and norepinephrine too fast which can cause a shortage in those vital neurotransmitters
4. A slow MAOA removes serotonin, dopamine and norepinephrine slower than normal which can leave you with an overabundance of those vital neurotransmitters.
5. Tryptophan and Riboflavin are 2 nutrients important to your MAOA gene

Recap of Chapter 9:

1. The main purpose of the GST gene is to produce the GST enzyme.
2. The GST enzyme helps your body transfer its primary detox agent, glutathione, to xenobiotics (such as heavy metals, herbicides, pesticides) so they can leave the body through your urine.
3. The main purpose of the GPX gene is to create the GPX enzyme.
4. The GPX enzyme helps your body convert hydrogen peroxide (produced when were under stress) to water so it can exit the body in your urine.
5. Cysteine, Riboflavin and Selenium are 3 nutrients important to your GST/GPX genes.

Recap of Chapter 10:

1. The main purpose of the NOS3 gene is to influence the creation of nitric oxide.
2. Nitric oxide is extremely important to heart health because it affects blood vessel formation and blood flow.

3. The main way your NOS3 gets dirty is chemical exposure.
4. To stay clean your NOS3 gene requires BH4, Arginine, Calcium, Iron, Riboflavin, oxygen and it helps a lot for your other genes to be clean as well.

Recap of Chapter 11:

1. The main job of the PEMT gene is the production of phosphatidylcholine.
2. Phosphatidylcholine's job is to keep your cell membranes healthy and fluid which lets them operate at their peak level.
3. Without its membrane your cell dies, if you remove the nucleus from a cell it will live a while longer but if the membrane is removed it dies fast.
4. Vegans and vegetarians are at a much higher risk of being choline deficient.
5. Research has proven that mothers who consumed greater levels of choline while pregnant had babies with improved learning abilities and improved memories while mothers who lacked choline while pregnant tended to have babies with decreased learning abilities and decreased memory

Recap of Chapter 12:

1. your weight gain, insomnia, rashes and headaches are caused by dirty genes and simply taking pills doesn't fix the problem, it just puts a band-aid on it
2. Hunger is when your stomach growl's and feels empty and you know you need to eat. Cravings are a feeling that you want to eat a specific item

3. Nutrients are often lost due to temperature extremes, the cooking process and even transportation.
4. The easiest form of supplements for your body to absorb is liquid, the hardest is tablets
5. Check for toxins like mold or mildew, Look for damp areas and water spots on the ceiling or floor, and be sure to clean up and remove any found
6. Try improving the quality of your sleep by not eating 3 hours before bedtime, turning off any lights, drinking no caffeine after 2pm, stopping any electronic activity an hour before bedtime and perhaps instill a blue light filter for your phone or computer.
7. Try some deep breathing exercises. There are many free app's, android and apple, that will walk you through guided meditation or breathing exercises.

Recap of Chapter 13:

1. If you want food to be your medicine then you must eat healthy, supportive and clean foods.
2. Use only filtered water when cooking and buy only organic ingredients for cooking.
3. Typical fish, meats and produce will only make your genes dirty just like unfiltered water.
4. You should be using Celtic or Himalayan sea salt instead of regular table salt. These 2 alternatives are high in minerals

Recap of Chapter 14:

1. The purpose of the second laundry list is to find out which of your genes need further attention, spot cleaning, and which are doing better.
2. You should only be completing the second laundry list if you've already done the 2 week soak and scrub.

3. Try to form some new habits, better habits, by revisiting this second laundry list every 6 months or so to give your genes a quick checkup.

Recap of Chapter 15:

1. You shouldn't start the spot cleaning until after you've completed the soak and scrub.
2. In order for the spot clean to work all your genes need to be pretty clean. This is important because genes work together in clusters and groups
3. If you still notice trouble spots you might want to reach out to a qualified professional such as a functional medicine professional, a licensed naturopathic physician or an environmental medicine professional

About High Speed Reads

Here at High Speed Reads our goal is to save you time by providing the best summaries possible.

If you learned something beneficial from this book then I'd like to ask you a favor, would you be kind enough to leave a review on Amazon? It would be greatly appreciated. Lastly, if you haven't yet make sure you purchase Dirty Genes as this summary is meant to complement it, not replace it.

Thanks so much and good luck on your journey to better health.

Made in the USA
Las Vegas, NV
09 February 2023